ON A WHI'

*A Memoir of Love, Loss
and the Healing Power of Art*

by Cathy Phelan-Watkins

Published by Clink Street Publishing 2018

ISBN:
978-1-912850-04-4- paperback
978-1-912850-05-1 - ebook

PROLOGUE

"He walks away, the sun goes down"
Amy Winehouse, Tears Dry On Their Own

Three in the morning and I'm wide, wide awake. My head is spinning. I'm anxious, panicking. "I need to put it all together. To catch it before it all slips away again." I did try and sleep after a session with Ms Winehouse and Doctor Smirnoff but I have now accepted that sleep is not a possibility at this point.

I get out of bed. It's cold. I'm wearing an oversized t-shirt, dressing gown and a pair of climbing socks. I switch on a lamp. I look down onto the street outside. The tarmac is wet and inky, no foxes tonight. All is still and silent. I am on a mission. They have got to be here somewhere. All twenty-three of them. One for every year we were together.

I pour myself a slug of vodka and fill the glass to the brim with orange juice and some ice cubes from the kitchenette off the lounge. Maybe in that box? I drag a chair into the corridor, still clutching my drink. I clamber up, socked feet slipping. Try not to kill myself. I can't quite reach. The box I want is on top of another box. My fingertips are just touching it. A few pushes to the side and I have it. The box of Danny stuff. Letters, postcards and yes, a small bundle tied up with red ribbon. The Valentine's cards.

'Guess who?' 'I love you', 'Happy Valentine's Day gorgeous'. There are red hearts, pink hearts, red glitter, tiny hearts on strings. Some tasteful, some naff , maybe bought in a hurry from the corner shop. A Terry Frost painting. A yellow card with the words: 'to the world you may be one person but to me you are the world'. And the last one in which he has written 'halfway to heaven and already an Angel'. Strange. It's like reading them for the first time. Somehow I didn't appreciate the sweetness of his words before. It must be four o'clock now. I lay the cards in a line on the carpet. Mission accomplished. I am utterly exhausted, but temporarily at peace. Order has been restored in some tiny but important way. Welcome to my world.

Grief gets you like this. Three in the morning or three in the afternoon. Any time of day or night. The storm clouds can come, the waves can suck you under. Since my husband Danny died of bowel cancer three months ago, it is almost as if I have become a person of the sea. I sail in a tiny boat, adrift in the ocean, no dry land in sight. I am a poor navigator. A queasy instability prevails, even when my boat is becalmed. That and a constant need to dig down, to retrieve and stick it all together again. This need to bring him back.

I had got into a similar state of agitation, perhaps a week or two earlier. On that occasion it had been a desperation to find a photograph of a holiday in Cornwall. It was in the middle of the night again. I'd got up, and put Amy Winehouse on – Back to Black, of course – as I rifled through boxes and drawers. I'd found the photo in the office upstairs. There we had been, sitting on a rock in the sunshine. Him in the Arran sweater with no elbows. Myself beaming. Happy times.

There can be relief in finding anything now. Nail clippers, half-used packets of Rennie in the pockets of winter coats or rucksacks. Sometimes I strike gold by finding a scrap of paper with his handwriting. Numbers, scribbles, his distinctive doodles, shopping lists and funny faces – even a pack of pre-signed Christmas cards, ready to send. These scraps of paper have become as intimate to me as a touch or a warm breath. A previously unseen photograph assuming the power of a resurrection.

The next morning I am tired but okay. I am sitting in the blue stripy armchair from the British Heart Foundation shop in Brixton. The one I bought for Danny when he was ill, in a desperate attempt to find a piece of furniture that didn't offend his increasingly frail skeleton. It is placed in the very spot where he died. Where he left the planet. I experience a distinct and special charge when I sit here. It's not at all depressing, quite the opposite. I find it positive. Empowering. I have come to think of it as the 'beam me up chair' – perhaps one day, like Captain Kirk and Danny, I will find myself transported to another dimension.

Still in my dressing gown and t-shirt, I view the collection of Valentine's cards on the carpet from this position, moving them about with my toes. I count them. Twenty-two. There should be twenty-three. "Where is the other one? Could it have been the first one? Have I thrown it away? Had he forgotten one year?" I am distracted by a small stack of postcards, mementoes of our most precious holidays. "When did that happen? When did we go there and when did we do that?" It's all getting rather jumbled and I am starting to feel distressed again. I need to sort it out before I start to forget. Before I lose it.

I start to pace up and down in the living room still looking at the irregular line of cards. "What if I arranged them on a length of paper? Wallpaper, perhaps. Created a testament. A scroll. A visual timeline." For a moment I feel the familiar, affirming cogs, grind into life. Calibrations. Questions. For the first time in more than a year, proper artistic ones. "Would it work as a piece? And if so, how? Against what background? On what scale?" I feel part of me restoring itself. Switches within me, trip on. "Is this how I am going to cope? How I am going to make sense of it all?" Through art.

Part One

SKELETON

Two days to Christmas. The staff of the publishing company that Danny founded have left for their ten-day holiday, so the office is empty apart from the chief executive, Julian. Danny last set foot in this building more than a year and a half ago. Having spent twenty-five years building up the company, I can only imagine – or perhaps I can't imagine – how the dawning realisation of never returning to this, the 'engine room' of his life, must have affected him.

I spent yesterday painting the boardroom, or to be precise the room we use for meetings. The damp patch on the wall had become depressing. The woodwork had started to look scuffed, careworn. I have given it all a fresh lease of life. Bright white. The paint has now dried and I am rearranging the furniture. I have decided to hang the black and white photo that we used at the memorial service here. It is a heavy object and possibly a little large for the room. I lift it into place and drill the appropriate holes for the screws. I want him to be here.

The portrait depicts Danny, resplendent in one of his pin-striped suits from Sidney Charles, his old tailor in Deptford High Street. The picture was taken some years ago. The suit is old-fashioned, with that high lapel favoured by Paul Smith in the early nineties. The stripe is more than a little too wide for now. Think Del-boy/Wall Street banker, then mix with something Irish and engagingly handsome, and you are probably there. He looks good but it doesn't make me feel as good as I had hoped.

I glance at the clock on the opposite wall. It's dark outside already, the wind is rattling the metal shutters. "Better get going or I'll miss B&Q," I say to Julian.

I want to buy some materials before they close for the holiday. I have turned down invitations to stay with friends because I want to spend Christmas – my first Christmas since Danny's death last February – in the studio. Alone. The numerous invitations I received from friends were no doubt sincerely offered and definitely gratefully received.. Nevertheless, something inside me knows that I do not want to experience some else's Christmas. I want my own Christmas.

It is more than six months since I toyed with making a piece incorporating all the Valentine's cards. It turned out to be a blind alley. I assembled something, an arrangement of the cards on a long piece of wallpaper, but it wasn't going to work. I realised it had been an impulse, a reaction to that feeling that our whole life together had been lost. I had simply wanted to retrieve and preserve it. Creativity has to be about more than that.

Other ideas had come and gone. At one point I'd thought about making a travel bag. I imagined applying an assortment of patches and badges, marking our holidays together, to some kind of fabric structure. A bag, a quilt perhaps? A way of celebrating good times. Italy. Spain. Cornwall. Barbados. We both worked hard, so the holidays we had together meant a lot. They were very special to us although never long enough. That idea didn't linger either.

The immense pressure of sorting everything out and coping with the grief of others as much as my own, had prevented me from doing anything creative. Weeks had passed without me finding the energy to set foot in the studio. This was something that I had always thought unimaginable. I felt like I had lost touch with that side of me, with the person – the artist – I was before Danny's illness. Lack of sleep also was a factor. So now, I am excited if slightly nervous. I have an idea that I feel I can pursue. I need to buy some wood. The weather is grim and getting worse. I don't drive, so the journey may require me to take a couple of buses, at least. I may even need to visit more than one store. It is an inexact science. I won't know what I want until I see it. But then, I do, right there. "Danny. Is this you?" I think.

Outside the office next door, there is a loose stack of discarded wood propped up haphazardly against the wall. I look more closely. Carpet runners. Mostly long, around a metre or a metre and a half, but also some shorter lengths. Some broken, snapped pieces. They must have been ripped out during the office refurb next door. They've got the tacks in them still, but I can remove those. How do I carry them back to the house?

I nip back into the office and find a bit of string so that I can bind them up. I try to explain what I am doing to Julian. From the way he looks at me, I suspect he thinks I have lost the plot completely. I tuck the bundle under my arm and set off home. Other people walk past with bags of supermarket shopping, clinking with bottles of wine, wrapped presents. One young guy is hauling a Christmas tree.

The wind comes in gusts, catching the flimsily bound wood. The icy rain angles in and I am forced to readjust the bundle. It's hard to avoid the sharpness of the tacks. I am pleased nevertheless. Thrilled, in fact. I drop the runners on the floor of the studio downstairs.

Thanks Danny. I won't do any work tonight. I am an early bird. At my best, first thing. I will get started tomorrow morning, Christmas Eve. I go upstairs and try to watch TV, but can't. Too many thoughts again.

It is strange. Danny's presence is so elusive, like a slippery bar of soap. I did not feel it at all hanging his portrait. Yet as I sit here, a damp blanket of seasonal gloom hugging the studio, he feels close again. In a good way. At times like this, he can come to me in a crazy carousel of images. Scattergun hits on targets across a quarter of a century. Like a drunk driver, I can lurch from visions of us walking through the scented pine forests of Formentera, to drinking rum in downtown Barbados. And then at another moment, he is struggling – and failing – to keep his composure on a desperate day at the Royal Marsden Hospital. From there I can be flipped back, to him sitting blissfully on the clifftops of Pendeen in Cornwall.

Tonight, with Christmas so close, the images are almost themed. Laughing uncontrollably on a crazy December break in Barcelona. We had brought a Christmas pudding with us and had given it to the hotel chef to heat up. It had come back as Christmas soup. And then returning to our place in Cornwall, after a walk on Christmas morning. Thoroughly oxygenated and ready to tear into the turkey. More recently, him sitting, wincing with pain on the last Christmas we had spent in St Ives. That had been the calm before the storm. Before the beginning of the cancer journey. The beginning, of the end.

We had spent that Christmas 2014 largely housebound, denied our normal clifftop walks by my flat feet. Well, damaged tendons, to be more precise. It had been frustrating. The weather had been crisp and sunny. From the window of our living room and kitchen I'd looked out on stunning, eggshell-blue skies. While Danny had busied himself clearing leaves and assorted other chores in the garden, I'd made up for the disappointment by cooking. A rather good turkey stew and a particularly pleasing version of my Christmas cake, a Delia Smith recipe with treble quantities of brandy.

There had also been lots of television. Old films mostly. A 1970s version of *The 39 Steps* with Robert Powell and one of my favourites, *Force 10 from Navarone*, with Edward Fox and Robert Shaw. It had been filmed in the old Yugoslavia and reminded us of an extraordinary train journey we had made through the mountains from Ploce on the Bosnian coast to Sarajevo only the summer before. I think the train had been donated by the Swedish government possibly after the war. Seated in the stylish but rather uncomfortable wood-panelled carriages, we had sped through the densely forested landscape, minarets alternating with church spires at every turn in the track, while our fellow travellers, mainly locals, chain-smoked with gusto, leaving us to compete for any available oxygen.

Our recent burst of travel had been deliberate, our reaction to a nagging suspicion that Danny needed to address his health and to slow down a little. The previous year had been particularly stressful for him and he'd become severely exhausted. He'd also experienced twinges of stomach pain for which he'd sought advice. I still have the letter from a top consultant reassuring him that he was 'a well man'. We'd put the intermittent discomfort that followed down to a variety of other ailments. Irritable bowel syndrome? A gluten allergy?

Ironically we'd wilfully ignored a bowel cancer awareness campaign on television at the time. I remember the strapline, it was something about having blood in your poo. All faintly embarrassing to watch in your living room and for us not relevant. Danny was not experiencing those symptoms. Our logic had been as lazy as it had been pig-ignorant. "If it is a tumour the discomfort would be present all the time." "Perhaps it is some form of food poisoning or a rather persistent stomach virus?" As had been the case with a friend of ours in Cornwall. The experience had, however, made Danny at last begin to toy with the idea of a change in his working life. To ease off after twenty-five years in the saddle running his publishing company. And so we made a decision. It was time to have more fun, more holidays.

The issue appeared to have gone away but then after Christmas, Danny began to feel unwell. At first I'd wondered if it was simply seasonal over-consumption but after a few days it was clear that there was something amiss. He had grown increasingly uncomfortable.

On New Year's Eve, he had sat on a chair in the middle of the living room silent, not eating, then slid off to bed for a few hours before reappearing at midnight to watch the annual fireworks from the window. As ever it was spellbinding. Smeaton's Pier across the bay had taken on the appearance of an Elizabethan galleon in battle. As the last spray of stars had evaporated into the night sky, we had headed off to bed, determined to catch the first train back to London the next morning.

Once home, Danny would not eat. I made him a very thin chicken broth to no avail. Not even a bowl of Frosties could tempt him. I had implored him to go back to our GP, but he ducked the issue, preferring to book an appointment with an acupuncturist. It was the middle of the first week of January when he woke me first thing one morning to tell me that he was going to the surgery at Camberwell Green. I was groggy, half asleep, but relieved. He had been gone for no more than an hour when he phoned to say he was in an ambulance on his way to A&E.

It's early December 2015. After almost a year and a half of abstinence there is no escaping my need to get back to my art. People always think that artists must have very strong personalities. I would say it is quite the opposite. I think we either come from problematic backgrounds, or have a fragile, indistinct sense of self. Part of the same thing. A feeling of being alien. And so the act of making something, is a way to assert yourself. To mediate between the world and yourself. Something to bridge the internal and the external. That could involve any number of extraordinary actions, from painting a sunset to videoing a bit of dust floating in the air. There are easier ways to lead a life and to 'fit in'. Especially as you get older. But...

I have to do something with all these feelings I have. And so I have decided to create a sculpture of a horse. A great, big, beautiful, monumental, heroic horse.

The idea has been brewing away for a few weeks now. It began with a feeling that I wanted to do something to celebrate Danny. Monumentalise him. Because he was a very exceptional man and I am concerned that he wasn't celebrated enough. He didn't play that game. There was also something about filling a physical space. A space that he no longer occupied.

I was struck by the idea of an heroic structure, the sort of thing that generals and other military heroes are remembered with – hewn out of chunks of marble on the streets of the world's capital cities. The mark of a great man. Aware of the irony I also knew that it couldn't be a pure representation of him sitting astride some magnificent steed. I wouldn't want to do that, to make a likeness of him or some kind of pastiche.

But then it occurred to me that this was about absence as well. His absence. "So what if it is just the horse? Yes. That will work." A mythical, heroic horse. Perhaps it could be Prince Charming's horse. Because, he was after all the nearest I could get to such a figure in my life.

I am remembering a big white horse carved on a hill from my childhood. I must have visited it on a school trip. Bronze age I think. I am curious about the spiritual resonance of white horses. What do they mean? A quick google search gives me some answers. The horse on the hill might have been the Uffington horse in Oxfordshire? Its purpose to this day is unknown. Apparently it was cut out by Celtic followers of the horse goddess Epona who rode a white mare to escort souls to the land of the dead.

In Paleolithic times, white horses were symbols of the connection between the everyday world and the afterlife. Then there are the winged horses employed by the Valkyrie of the Norse to collect the spirits of heroes fallen in battle. Let's not forget Pegasus, one of the most recognised creatures in Greek mythology. Conduit of thunder and lightning and fountain head of wisdom for the poets. White horses were highly prized sacrificial animals in Hindu culture also, being the preferred ride of many of Vishnu's incarnations. Generally the white horse would appear to represent a force of triumph over evil and in many cases the means to transcend this world.

There was also an unusual print hanging in our house when I was a child. It was of St George and the Dragon by Uccello. Probably purchased from the National Gallery, or it may even have been some kind of calendar. I decide to look that up too on my computer. Uccello about 1470. The image depicts an episode from a popular collection of saints' lives written in the thirteenth century. George is defeating the dragon while the chinless wonder of a princess is waiting to bring the beast to heel with her belt. The horse is gleaming white, beautiful and sturdy, if a little awkwardly placed. It is rearing up on its hind legs resplendent in a scarlet saddle and bridal. The tail is artfully coiffured like a 1930s perma-wave. The dragon is an ugly frog-coloured creature with circular target shapes on its wings. It stands on splayed reptilian feet with sharp talons. Monstrous. Invasive. Alien.

I continue searching. Another Uccello pops up. *The Battle of San Romano*. This is a stunning painting. Men at war on horseback with lances. It is a very complex image with some

25

intriguing attempts at perspective. Two white horses dominate. Both rearing on their hind legs, facing each other. Clearly a useful pictorial device, setting up a strong tonal contrast with the dark colours of the black horses and the foliage behind. I don't know, but I would be prepared to bet that the guys on the white horses are winning. At this point I must make it clear that I am not a 'horsey' person. Nor was I one of those little girls who worshipped horses. If I had a preferred animal, it would have been a cat. Right now however, it's all about white horses. But why?

Perhaps there is something about how we retain symbols that is not unlike how we might hold on to the rudiments of a foreign language. Words and phrases redundant ordinarily, just waiting to be called to arms at the appropriate time. When something needs to be said. Visual references work like this for me. Buried deep in some far corner of my consciousness, there are libraries of images. Not organised in any way that I could describe, but available for use when required. The process of retrieval at any given time, is a bit of a mystery.

I become aware of a tune that has been worming away in my head for days. What is it? There was a TV series a long time ago. Well it must have been a while because it was in black and white. It was in a foreign language, about a girl and her Uncle Dimitri. And yes importantly, it was all about horses. I was obsessed by it. I can't quite remember the lyrics . Something about white horses and far away.

Yes, it has to be a white horse.

I wake up early on Christmas Eve. I make the first coffee of the day and head straight down to the kitchen. The house is a cold, crumbling wreck. On days like this, the basement assumes an almost subterranean quality. I can hear drips of water resonating from distant places. I watch the legs of passers-by at street level through the barred windows and yet I feel marooned as if on the sea bed.

The house had been the offices of Danny's publishing business, now relocated to more modern premises off Clapham High Street. It had lain empty for a number of years awaiting redevelopment until we moved in a few months after Danny's diagnosis. He insisted on this move, despite my reservations. Always one step ahead, always planning. It was the right decision, although I didn't think so at the time.

It is a Georgian flat-fronted block of a building.

Somewhat past any notions of splendour and sadly stripped of any period detail through decades of office use. Last decorated in the nineties in rather cold pastel colours, the carpet is worn and spotted with a patina of spilt coffees and downtrodden Blu-tac. Room after room revealing nothing more than a cluttered array of cheap office furniture. Manuals, magazines and out-of-date directories cluster in the corners of bookshelves. The unforgiving strip lighting in direct conflict with any sense of domesticity one might wish to achieve. I don't much like it, or the area, but the studio is its saving grace and I now realise, a key part in Danny's masterplan for the future. Or to be precise, my future.

Built in the 1890s as a workspace for the production of army supplies, it is a large, sprawling space backing on to a small patch of garden. It has windows the length of one wall. I had enjoyed using it as a studio for a couple of years previously while the building was empty. It's currently filled with various examples of my work. Paintings and sculptural pieces. Bits of bric-a-brac that I will one day use. Or not, as the case may be. An antique pram. A trampoline.

The broken carpet runners remain where I had left them the night before. I have spent the past hours working out how I am going to use them to create an armature, a structure upon which I will build the horse. I know that I need to solve two immediate problems. I intend the sculpture to be large. So I need the piece to be mobile, otherwise I won't be able to work on it. With this in mind, I have found a pallet on wheels. I think it was used for moving heavy boxes of magazines and paper around back in the day. I will construct the horse on it.

My other challenge is to achieve an anatomical accuracy. A believable horse. There was a time when Clapham Old Town would have had its share of drays and police horses, but those days have gone. Having no access to the real thing, I am resigned to using a toy or a model of some kind. I just want to be precise. It can't be any horse, of course. I need it to be fit for purpose and worthy of Prince Charming. A suitably dramatic and romantic animal.

I have a particular horse in mind. As a child I had a rich friend who had a Barbie doll and all the paraphernalia that came with it, including a magnificent horse and stable set. To my eyes, it was the most glamorous and exotic thing I'd ever seen. A few nights ago I had headed to Hamleys and to my annoyance they didn't have it. After some rooting around I found some other candidates, and in particular some beautifully crafted model horses. I eventually bought one; a six-inch black plastic horse. (The sales spiel on the box couldn't have been more apt. 'My Dream Horse' – Create Your Own.) My task now is to use the proportions and outline and scale it up by, I think, at least ten times. Easy for the math.

I begin by taking precise measurements and then attaching some of the carpet batons to the platform to form a very loose armature. I bind the structure together using brown luggage tape. I face an immediate problem: it keeps falling over. So I get two chairs and place them on the platform so that it can stand up. It looks fine. I'm certain the key measurements are correct.

I replace the two chairs temporarily with a spindly camera tripod. It is still standing. "Thank God."

I am sitting on my old, leather swivel chair – my Mastermind chair – looking at the rough, spindly armature that is taking shape, when I see it. I want the horse to tell our story and it is doing so already. The shattered, splints of wood have been bound together to form a skeleton. They are the bones, the strands of bound tape are the ligaments. It occurs to me that this is what Danny became towards the end. His once tall, healthy frame, reduced to eight and a half stone.

I see that I am trying to reverse the process. To flesh him out in some way.

The days and weeks following our return from that last Christmas in Cornwall had been a mess. A chaos of confusing diagnoses. Danny had been sent back from A&E with nothing more than codeine for the pain relief. The limited examination they'd conducted had been very inconclusive. The tablets, next to useless. The next morning he'd gone back to our GP in considerable pain. This time he was admitted to hospital for more extensive tests. There was clearly something wrong.

I was relieved that, at last, it was being taken seriously and he was going to have a proper examination, but inevitably, my mind was working overtime. After settling him in to his bed at King's Hospital, I popped in on some friends in Camberwell. Mary-Jane and Owen. I remember saying repeatedly that I hoped we were not about to start on a 'cancer journey'. Denial is everyone's default. Deep down, I think I knew what was about to unfold.

Danny remained in hospital until the eleventh of January, undergoing numerous tests and observations. Potential diagnoses for his symptoms were floated by the many and various consultants in circulation. Briefly hovering over his bed from time to time, they said little before wandering off. An image of exotic dragonflies jumping from one lily pad to another springs to mind. As if we were in a pool; we were the pond life.

He was reasonably comfortable in hospital but as soon as he returned home it was obvious again that he wasn't right. He still had no appetite and could manage little beyond the ubiquitous bowl of Frosties. He developed severe constipation and I was obliged to make several trips to all-night chemists for medication to combat the pain. All the signs were pointing to some kind of blockage in his stomach. We googled the symptoms endlessly. Hernia. Colitis. Appendicitis. Spastic colon. IBS. And, yes, of course, bowel cancer.

By 3 pm on the Sunday his pain was getting out of hand. I called a taxi to take us back to A&E. Fortunately it was not too crowded and he was administered with effective painkillers within twenty-five minutes. Unbeknown to me, I had been introduced to the world I was going to inhabit for the next year. And to my new role in life – rookie triage nurse.

Things then proceeded at a different pace, as if this great slumbering beast, the NHS, had at last woken up and began to fully engage with us. The next day, Monday, he was operated on. We were told that they were going to remove a tumour in his small intestine. The following few days were a seesaw of hope and despair. As ever in the dynamic of our relationship, we were at opposite ends of the seesaw. Me, cup half full, Danny swathed in Celtic gloom. His cup, as ever, half empty.

Life on the crowded ward was not without many interesting diversions. Here was South London in all its diversity and splendour. In the bed next to Danny, a large Nigerian family had gathered around their father in nonstop party mode, dispensing love and food in equal measure. It was all rather wonderful apart from the fact the flimsy cubicle curtains made it impossible to provide any sense of privacy for Danny or myself. Across the aisle, a blind man had, after ten days, been provided with a radio. In the corner, a desperate young man was under 24/7 guard after his umpteenth suicide attempt. Apparently he had jumped from a multi-storey car park, again. Danny spent his days recording it all in one of his infamous black notepads. Good and bad.

The post-operational pain was acute and Danny had been prescribed morphine. At one point – as high as a kite – he became convinced that he was blazing down some freeway in the States on a Harley-Davidson with some Hell's Angels. I was in no rush to bring him down from this fantasy – for his sake or mine. My primary emotion at this juncture was relief that the operation had gone smoothly and that whatever was causing the problems had been removed. But as the days passed, we developed a distinct sense that all was not quite right. Consultants avoided us. One random medic muttered 'carcinogenic' under her breath as she walked past. And then out of the blue, a swarm of white coats descended on us, rearranging the curtains in a flurry around Danny's bed as best they could.

The head honcho was pleasant enough, although worryingly for an expert in gastroenterology, he sported one of those male pregnancy-type beer guts. It was a testament to many – probably expensive – years of drinking and eating the wrong food. With what appeared to be a large grin on his face, he informed us that the surgeon had not been able to remove the tumour and that the cancer had already spread from the small intestine to the stomach lining.

Danny and I simultaneously reverted to type. I asked about the possibility of a treatment. A cure. Danny asked "How long have I got?" The answer came quickly enough.

"Four to six weeks." Danny passed out.

I'm not sure how my feet carried me home that evening. The walk from King's Hospital to our house in Camberwell was short and familiar. Along De Crespigny Park Road. Three-quarters of a mile perhaps. But how did I get there? Perhaps I flew through the air ? Like one of those Chagall paintings with star-crossed lovers flying through cobalt blue skies? Perhaps I dematerialised and reconstructed myself back in the empty living room? I have no recollection. No idea whatsoever.

Looking back on that evening I am astonished at how this news had been delivered to us. How the medics could dispense such horror without so much as a word of consolation or advice. Disappearing as they had arrived, with a flurry of something resembling bonhomie and another flap of that awful plastic curtain.

By chance, Danny's sister Sarah had been there too. We watched speechless as the nurses swabbed his clammy face and wheeled him to another ward. There was nothing we could do. Back at her home, Sarah had undoubtedly begun phoning around the family. I don't recall phoning or communicating with anyone. I couldn't have done that anyway. To verbalise the situation would have been to acknowledge it. I was simply not capable of doing that.

No one knows how they are going to react in extremis. In my case, a weird and defiantly prosaic practicality took over. I had to organise stuff to take to the hospital the next day. Paperwork, Tupperware. I did the washing up. A case of 'batten down the hatches'. There was a storm approaching.

The next morning I was shocked to find the contents of various cupboards in the living room strewn on the floor. For a split second, I thought there had been a burglary. But no, hang on, that was me. Like a woman possessed, I had started to 'pack up'. Emptying, removing, tidying up bits and pieces in a futile effort to gain control of a monstrous chaos.

In that very cold light of the next day I could feel that everything had changed.

Our home full of stuff, full of evidence of our lives together, had suddenly been transformed from a living stage to a collection of objects. All life removed, the breath sucked out, meaningless. Game over.

Part Two
MUSCLE

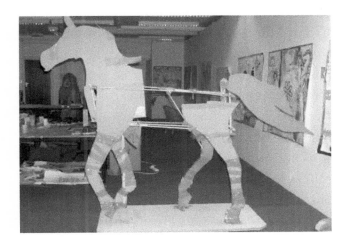

It's strange to think it now, but I'd almost ignored him. It was 1992 and I'd agreed to go out for an after-work – or to be precise – an after-show drink with my fellow dressers from the London Palladium where I had been working. This nightly commitment was one of three jobs I had taken on in order to fund my artistic ambitions. The other components of my patchwork employment portfolio consisted of cleaning the already spotless house of an Italian lady in Dulwich village and collecting a five-year-old from school, also in Dulwich. Back in the day it was possible to get by in this way, although finding the rent for my room in Greenwich could sometimes be a struggle.

It had been one of my workmates, Helen, who had persuaded me to join her and some others for a drink. I think it was her birthday. She'd mentioned her brother would be there too. I'd resisted at first. The nocturnal habits of theatre folk were dangerous. The last curtain call was often the beginning of a long night of after-hours drinking. I'd been tempted too often and been out too many nights already that week – a habit that was of course ruinous to any artistic momentum I might be striving for. On this occasion a combination of fatigue and a need for some company tipped the balance and I accepted the invitation. Against my better judgement.

Arriving at the pub, I'd sat next to a girlfriend, Christine. She was always fun, and often very loud. Helen's brother Danny had been sitting on the other side of me. He was wearing green tracksuit bottoms and a decidedly scruffy checked shirt. He looked tired, exhausted in fact. Head in his hands, he seemed to be exercised or stressed about something. He looked like he might be hard work so I'd given him a bit of a wide berth.

At some point in the evening there had been a moment when I'd had a choice. Keep speaking to the lively friend on one side or make contact with the stressed-out-looking guy on the other? It was like that movie, *Sliding Doors*, it could have gone either way. More out of politeness than anything else, I decided to give him a few minutes. If he was dull or depressing I could turn back to Christine or head home. What did I have to lose?

I can't remember how I started the conversation. Perhaps I asked him about himself, or more likely I fired a bit of Christine's craziness in his direction. It was as if a light had been switched on. And yes, that thing you read about in badly written books happened. Our eyes met and suddenly there was no one else in the room. We seemed to hit it off immediately. Within minutes we were discussing the possibility of driving across America together. Coast to coast. In a Thunderbird. He was very charming. Tall, handsome and intelligent. He told me he was stressed about the business he had just started. He was a publisher of some kind, working in the charity sector. It sounded interesting but meant little to me at that point. What was more intriguing was that he had previously been part of the management team looking after a band called Killing Joke. Not my kind of music but exciting nevertheless. Dangerous perhaps? There was also something about him. An energy and a warmth. He was quietly charismatic. It also turned out that his first marriage had broken up, which helped explain why he seemed to be carrying rather a heavy load emotionally.

The next day my flatmates perceived that something of significance had happened when they found me slumped on the sofa watching *Songs of Praise* in something of a daze. Who was he? Was it serious? Were we going to move in together? There seemed little prospect of that, but after this first encounter we started seeing each other. It was difficult to carve out much time together what with my deeply unsociable working hours and his rarely having any free time at all. There was however no question in my mind that this was serious.

Part of the attraction lay in the fact that we were interested in what each other did. He loved the fact that I was an artist. He collected paintings and when we subsequently went to galleries and exhibitions together, I discovered that he had a good eye. I was equally fascinated by his world. I had never met a publisher or even a businessman before. He was solvent which was something of a novelty for me. Definitely not the norm amongst the emerging artistic fraternity.

People meeting us might have seen two very opposite characters, yet we were alike in a lot of ways. We were both driven for a start. Danny was hugely defined by his childhood. He grew up as the second son of a large Irish family in Acton, west London. Housing was short after the war and at one point the entire family lived in two rooms with an outside toilet and no hot water. Eventually rehoused in a brand new council maisonette in Hillingdon, Danny often recalled his amazement on discovering the stairs. I think his drive was born out of his innate intelligence and also a desire to escape material deprivation. "Never apologise, never explain" was an oft'-repeated mantra. I of course had my art, which provided me with a similar focus and also stemmed from the particular nature of my childhood.

We'd moved in together shortly after our first holiday – a week in Crete. Our stay in a breeze-blocked basement that stunk overwhelmingly of the goats' toilet directly outside, could easily have been a disaster. Happily the geometry of our relationship had solidified; our apparent difference providing the glue. An introvert by nature, I was beguiled by Danny's fascination for people, no doubt furnished by his journalistic instincts. Thus my contentment to sit under a tree with a sketch pad was hugely enriched by his quest for knowledge and ability to communicate. On this trip specifically, the outpourings of the owner of the local raki bar provided a daily torrent of dramatic narrative. Heroic tails of resistance to the Nazis jostled with equally heroic descriptions of his mother and her daily ten-mile round trip from the village in the mountains to sweep out the fishermans' café in the bay. All of this on foot with a couple of toddlers in tow. Danny was the sort of person that people wanted to talk to. He had that kind of face.

We'd returned with an almost unspoken understanding that living together was the natural step. I'd demonstrated little resistance to leaving my shared accommodation, especially as Danny's house was in New Cross, barely a mile and a half away. I would still be able to hang out with my friends.

Danny at the time lived in the top three floors of a large late-Victorian pile just off Lewisham Way. Since the break-up of his marriage he had shared the premises with his youngest sister Sarah and Owen, an old school friend. The basement was occupied by a strange couple seemingly intent on creating a nuclear bunker – or was it free passage to Australia? Whatever the mission, the quantities of earth being excavated from underneath us provided a constant and sometimes acute sense of unease for us all.

Architecturally impressive, the dilapidated house wasn't exactly an upgrade for me. To put it bluntly, it was a tip. On close inspection it became evident that no horizontal or indeed vertical surface had been troubled with a duster or indeed any variety of cleaning fluid in recent times. The extent of disrepair is probably best summed up by a brief description of the communal bathroom.

A large room with a high ceiling, it overlooked a patchwork of gardens mostly neglected. The flooring consisted of very tired 1970s cork floor tiles liberally dotted with intricate arrangements of black growths. Clearly something to be avoided, especially with bare feet. There was a small bath replete with a rusting shower head capable of a singular dribble on a good day. Beside this was a shower cubicle which I christened the 'diphtheria unit' and declined to enter. Ever. There was a black and white TV plugged in on top of a washing machine, conveniently, all accessible from the bath. To add to the luxury it was possible to recline on an ancient velvet-covered chaise lounge, provided the can of Dulux was positioned correctly where the fourth leg should have been. Mysteriously every inch of cupboard space was filled to the brim with plastic bags.

From time to time I attempted to assert some gentle order or some upgrade, in the form of a bath mat, perhaps? Or the removal of – in my opinion – unnecessary plastic bags. In retrospect I should have realised that energy spent in this way was never going to achieve the desired result. Sometimes acceptance is a better option.

It's fair to say that prior to meeting Danny, I was finding life a little difficult. Quite tough in fact. I'd left Goldsmiths Art College in south London in 1984. The most celebrated of my peers, that generation of talent imaginatively named Young British Artists and led by Damien Hirst, were blazing a trail and becoming international superstars. Literally. I wasn't on the inner circle but had benefited from having been in their orbit. I had my first exhibition a few months before my twenty-first birthday at the Nicola Jacobs gallery in Cork Street, followed shortly after by a one woman show at The Photographers' Gallery. Over the next few years I built up a reasonably impressive CV exhibiting in what were considered the 'hot spots' of the day.

Despite what I can now recognise as having achieved some considerable success, I had no confidence and saw myself as a failure. By the early nineties my poor self-image and lack of income had started to crystallise. I was struggling. I didn't have a gallery or enough money to work on anything ambitious. Whilst I continued to work on creative projects on a daily basis, life had become an exhausting and often depressing routine of low-paid work and ever-decreasing self-worth. One particularly bleak night springs to mind. I had got off the train after working in town. It was dark, cold and wet. I can remember walking down Greenwich High Street thinking "This is too hard. Just too hard. I'm not sure I can do it anymore."

I had for some time been clinging on to my raison d'être with increasing difficulty. The purpose being, as it is for any committed artist, to communicate. In my case, this meant exhibiting my paintings somehow, somewhere. Rather inconveniently and in marked contrast to my fellow alumni, I was painfully shy and incapable of 'working the room' to my advantage or indeed committing any other form of self-promotion. In the presence of useful or powerful individuals I would, without fail, revert to a kind of artistically defined version of Tourette's. This unfortunate characteristic was in no way indicative of a lack of belief in my work. It was entirely symptomatic of my attitude to authority/establishment figures and the business of seeking approval. From my position as something of a self-elected outsider, it was a challenge to fathom how I might actually exhibit my work. Enter Danny the entrepreneur.

In his working life, first in the music business and then as a publisher, Danny loved to nurture talent in others. With me, at first it was very much a matter of giving my confidence a boost. "What do you mean you can't?" Always gentle but with a razor-sharp insight into any situation, he assumed something of a managerial role for me. This was never in terms of influencing the content of what I wanted to produce artistically. He was interested in the platform, the mechanics of finding an audience.

And so I embarked on a new phase of my exhibiting career, staging 'pop-up' exhibitions in weird places, sometimes hiring spaces and at times dipping into the commercial and public gallery sectors. Danny, as always, ready to disrupt the status quo, to shake up the rather snobbish closed shop that was the gallery system. A case of no approvals sought or permissions required. That, and a large dose of his firm belief that there were no limits to what could be achieved. He was fearless in many ways.

On very rare occasions, the universe delivers. This was such a moment. I can see now that I was ready for a new beginning. Prince Charming had arrived just in time. Not exactly clad in shining armour or on a white charger. More a case of a cheap plaid shirt and a Ford Escort. I was definitely in a good place.

It's a 10 am on Christmas morning 2015. I am wrung out by the six-mile bicycle ride I have just undertaken from Clapham to Camberwell Cemetery, not far from Peckham Rye. It is raining incessantly. Looking north into the distance, the London skyscape is the colour of an iron pail. The ancient and modern spires of the City are a jagged blur, obscured by sheets of grey.

Behind me, the weather doesn't seem to be dampening the day's festivities which are already under way. A big estate car has pulled up outside one of the neat, Victorian terraced houses overlooking the graveyard and is being noisily emptied of children and presents. There's a dog too, barking excitedly. I wait for their hosts to welcome them all inside. I am not envious. I have chosen to be alone.

I have leaned my bike against a tree near a patch of grass where a simple wooden cross marks his resting place. It's still raining a bit more than a drizzle. I draw the hood of my anorak over my head and pull out the book of poetry I have brought with me. It is a collection designed to combat stress. Useful I thought, when I bought it.

Reading to Danny has become a ritual, a balm to me. Somehow to speak out loud is reassuring in itself. That and the fact that Danny loved poetry. It's not that I think he is here, but there again in a sense, he is everywhere now. Somehow the act of visiting the cemetery is hugely cathartic in a way I could never have imagined. As a person of no faith, I am beginning to understand something of the realm of pilgrimage. How deeply restorative it is to designate some time and thought in this way. Perhaps even more importantly, to express that in the form of a physical journey.

Today I have decided to read some Larkin. I read the poem 'An Arundel Tomb'. It is a bit morbid actually, but I am particularly moved by the last line 'What will survive of us is love'. At some point soon I am going to have to think about a permanent memorial. What to put on it? This might be an idea.

I have spent Christmas with Danny for the last 23 years, since I was in my twenties. This is the first one without him and I am more than determined to spend it alone. There is no moving me on this one, despite many offers gratefully received from friends and family. From my point of view, not to come to the cemetery would cause me immense distress. It would feel like an act of desertion on my part. That and giving myself the opportunity to cry if I want to, or indeed laugh. Loneliness is not the issue here. I just want to experience my own Christmas rather than someone else's. I want to feel what I feel, rather than make small talk over a mince pie. I have always hated mince pies anyway!

All that aside, I have happily accepted an invitation to visit one of Danny's oldest friends, Stuart, who lives in Greenwich. He and his wife Ros are going to a pub for Christmas lunch. I have decided I can cope with that. I think it will be comforting and fun. Provided I can visit the cemetery first and head home afterwards under my own steam.

I don't drive, so I have borrowed a bike from my neighbours, Debbie and Nigel. Imagining a leisurely tour of South London I was instead faced with slow muscle-burning hill climbs and incessant squally rain. Both the weather and my lack of fitness have conspired to present more of a challenge than I expected. As I wheel my bike back through the twisting lanes of the cemetery to the entrance gates, it's all starting to feel suitably melodramatic.

I am contemplating that word. Widow. A scary word, almost ludicrous. Not something

one ever aspires to, for sure. Thoughts of
The Merry Widow. Was that a fifties musical?
Maybe I should vamp it up in black lace and
a pencil skirt. All around me blotchy cherubs
twang on harps. Slabs of limestone form
variegating angles to the soft earth like newly-
sprung arrows. A crumbling gothic splendour
prevails. I think of that most powerful residue
of widowhood, Queen Victoria, with her bell-
shaped scowl. I can remember in the weeks
directly after Danny died, diverting myself with
the fantasy of sweeping around Sainsbury's
in a black crinoline. It was something about
playing it out. An attempt to occupy the word,
widow. I think of football teams wearing black
armbands, of other cultures and times where
I might have been able to express what I am
feeling outwardly. To let the world know.

I am in a foreign land – or is it a minefield?
There is that awful moment, that split second
when you wake up. Before you remember.
The blazing sunshine before the deluge. Then
everything crowds in once more and reality
has created its own cage. The saddest times are
often provoked by occasions when I could be
experiencing joy. What to do when something
good happens? It strikes me that joy struggles
to exist in the singular. The tree falls in the

forest and there is no one to notice, so the saying goes. Or is there?

There are also the spooky things that have happened since Danny's departure from this world. Things that I am way too embarrassed to mention to most of my friends, or at least those who have not experienced a major bereavement, and the madness that goes with it. I have a list of them in the back of my diary. A list of strange happenings. The favourite book that literally jumped off the book shelf. The teaspoon that propelled itself from a cake stand. The papier-mâché seagull that fell forward from a high shelf in response to me talking about the possibility of a male lodger moving in.

For the first six months I chose to understand all these strange physical occurrences as direct communications from Danny. Partly because I wanted to. I needed to. Now I am not so sure. But what about the incident of the Elton John track in the newsagent? I ask myself. This was on a visit to the cemetery earlier in the year. I was thirsty so I dropped into the newsagent next door to the main entrance to get a bottle of water. As I pushed open the door, there was a song blaring out on the radio. It was 'Daniel'. Of all the radio stations and all the tracks in the world it had to be that. Quite a coincidence for sure and something that in my grief-addled state, did give me a moment. Of what, I am not entirely sure.

Perhaps I would be wise to take heed of the message from the papier-mâché seagull. The one about men moving in. I discovered quite early on in my widowhood that along with many socially awkward and painful aspects, the condition also carries with it something of a sexual charge.

Imagine or recall what it is like to become single after the end of a relationship, then times by ten. So yes, there is the inevitable interest from male friends – single or otherwise – with becoming 'available', but there is something else going on too. Something ancient perhaps? A primeval sex/death equation to do with healing and probably the survival of the tribe. There must be books on this subject. If not there should be, because it was quite evident to me.

The needs of the tribe aside, I chose to regard these advances as a form of gallantry, aware also that I was undoubtedly emitting a rarefied energy myself. Some kind of post-traumatic stress/adrenaline-fuelled 'aliveness', which was clearly apparent not only to the male members of the tribe but to all and sundry. My friend Alice – also recently bereaved and single – experienced a similar phenomenon which she chose to describe as "like being famous". Strangely this did seem to sum it up quite well. At least it gave us both a bit of a lift through some dark times.

As I continue towards the big iron gates I stop to read some of the gravestones. I focus on ages particularly. Some, devastatingly young. Many men in middle age like Danny. I remind myself that it isn't just me dealing with this particular pain. I feel an enormous empathy with those interred here and for those grieving for them. I am definitely not alone.

Lunch with Stuart and Ros is generous and agreeably boozy. After the long return cycle ride, I get home early evening, exhausted. My legs hurt. I run a deep bath and just lie there, letting the lunchtime drinks wear off, my mind already turning back to the sculpture. I spend the rest of Christmas day calculating, planning. I go to bed excited, eager to press on and am up early the following day, straight in to the studio.

The first coffee of the day. I have butterflies in my stomach. This is what art can feel like. There are times for me particularly with sculpture, when the preamble is slow. Like an ache. Or perhaps an itch. A faint but indistinct knowledge that something is brewing. Festering. I plan. I pace around. There may be test drives. Sketches. Fine drawings. Experiments with colour and materials. Only then, when the time is right, will work commence. Art can be borne of the need to communicate anger too and this can be problematic. One step forward may be followed by two steps back. Too frenzied. But not this time. Not with this level of importance.

Now it is a compunction. An almost lemming-like drive to jump off a cliff. A need to release this stuff bottled up inside me. To resurrect my creative self. So I am pleased – not to say more than a little relieved – to find that the armature is still solid. I stress-test it. The joints seem firm. It has a stability, an equilibrium as it stands now. It can take some weight, I tell myself. It will need to.

I have dug out some huge bits of cardboard. Discarded boxes that have been stored away in readiness for moments like this. Along with several rolls of shiny brown packaging tape. That's often part of an artist's persona too, of course; the acquirer of flotsam and jetsam. The creative magpie.

I lay the brown sheets out on my table and begin to draw and then cut out the silhouette of the horse. It is broken into sections; four legs, the tail, the rump, hindquarters and the head. I have planned my measurements, extrapolating from the model horse. It has to be accurate. I cut out each section, then begin the slow process of attaching them to the armature, binding and strapping them on with tape. From time to time I sit on the Mastermind chair, swivelling from side to side, weighing up each addition from every angle. This is about much more than correctness. It cannot just be a convincing horse. It must have life. Energy. Abundant amounts of both. This is something about which I have been clear from the first genesis of the idea. For me the beauty of a static sculpture is about implied movement. You will find this throughout the centuries. From ancient Egyptian sculpture to the best of Elisabeth Frink. My horse must have this. It must be strong and vibrant. This cannot be a sad bereft animal. It has to be fit for a hero. It has to embody some magic.

I have a postcard of a horse's head. It is from the British Museum. I think it is exhibited in the 'Greeks in Italy' room. Just about life-size, it is carved out of a block of marble and supported by a metal rod. *"Once part of a much larger work, probably featuring a man and his horse"* so the blurb says. *"Frequently depicted in funerary contexts and used to emphasise the aristocratic roots of the deceased."* It is the colour of porridge. Nostrils flared, the skin ripples around the mouth. There are veins climbing up to the eyes which are blank yet all-seeing. The curly mane is parted neatly from the centre not unlike the coiffure of a Swiss schoolgirl. If you look at the horse long enough, it begins to breathe. This piece of marble is warm. I also have an image of horses on a vase. Depicted four deep in black on a deep rust colour. Elegant and highly stylised, the silhouetted sets of legs form a kind of fan shape, almost like the effect of those animated books where the drawn image appears to move as you flick the pages.

Then there are the horses from the Parthenon, also in the British Museum. The ones on the South Frieze are particularly vigorous. Sinuous muscle and pulsating veins, forming tangles of galloping limbs. I can hear the thud of their hooves on a dirt track. Eat your heart out Charlton Heston. There is something else in the main concourse of the museum which always stops me in my tracks. A beautiful statue of a youth on horseback. Roman, first century, apparently. It is very fine. Anatomically perfect and so detailed, down to the horse's teeth and the tie on the prince's sandals. The horse is standing on three legs with one of the front hooves raised off the ground. This is the exact pose of my plastic model.

My horse now has a shape or, to be more precise, a more articulated skeleton. I have added sections of chicken wire to essay the ribcage and breast bone. Now it's about muscle. I start to make fist-size spheres like snowballs from sheets of newspaper. Twenty, thirty, of them. The next bit of the task is tricky. How to attach the snowballs to the structure. Holding the brown sticky tape in my mouth I start to build up the torso starting with the area below the neck and working towards the rump. It is slow, rather precarious work. Think of a slow-motion Edward Scissorhands. Once sufficient bulk has been achieved in any one section, I bind the area together with a strapping of sticky tape. The surface is firm but springy and quite a good colour for a horse.

Over the next few days I run out of tape several times, necessitating frequent visits to the local DIY shop in Clapham High Street which thankfully doesn't recognise Christmas, apart from the excellent array of fairy lights and tree stands available. It is that peculiar period between Christmas and new year. South London is like a ghost town or a no man's land. All hostilities have ceased. There is space on the roads. I like the sense of otherness and possibility. All good for the task in hand.

I am working twelve-hour days and more. From time to time I stop for a cup of tea and a chance to warm up in the house. Gazing out of the window from the lounge I have begun to develop a little fantasy about the red post-box across the street. I imagine it as a button which once pressed might transport me to another dimension, another time and place.

Over the past year I have come to understand grief in no small part as a form of post-traumatic stress. I am easily spooked. A smell, a sound, an object, any person or thing has the capacity to trigger memories. Sometimes happy, but often distressing. The deepest pain lies in revisiting difficult moments. Unresolved issues. Failures that are exacerbated by the knowledge that they cannot be corrected. The relationship that was once a 'work in progress' now consigned to history. Set in stone. It can be the tiniest domestic detail that provides a trigger. I remember something and for the next six or seven hours I am in that tiny boat at sea again. Cut loose and unable to locate terra firma.

Recently, for instance, I became fixated by a painful memory of tidying up the garden together. Danny was picking up leaves and decanting them into one of those green garden refuse sacks. He wanted me to help. I could see the rainclouds gathering and was intent on finishing work on pruning the hedge. I refused to hold the bag open. He was cross. Hurt even. He went quiet. Why couldn't I have helped him? I should have been more flexible. Why couldn't we have done this one thing together?

It was something about his enjoyment of working with people versus my more solitary nature. My need for a certain amount of artistic isolation. This was a conflict of habit more than anything but so unnecessary – especially in the light of us having so little 'quality time' together. And now it's all over. I can't work on being more flexible or more understanding. It's too late. The pain I feel is immense, not least because there is absolutely nothing I can do to put it right.

Then there was the incident of the Christmas tree. It had been our first Christmas together in New Cross. I'd gone down to Lewisham and bought the biggest Christmas tree ever. I can't quite remember how I had got it home. Maybe I sequestered a shopping trolley or something because I don't drive and deliveries of such things didn't happen in those days. Finding an appropriately sized bucket, I had placed the tree in the middle of the living room. Then, risking life and limb standing on chairs and whatever was available I proceeded to decorate it. Bling, baubles, angels and chocolate. It was spectacular, albeit in a pound-shop kind of way. Once finished, I waited for Danny to return from work. It was Christmas Eve but ever the workaholic, he did not return until late.

"What do you think?" I said.

"Think of what," he'd replied.

"The f***ing tree."

He hadn't noticed it and yes, I was furious and baffled by his blindness in equal measure.

There were more serious issues. Some discussed. Some not discussed enough. I blame time-poverty. That and emotional cowardice on both sides. It's strange that it is in the recollection of the minutiae of our relationship that the pain lingers. Now I have to let go. The time has run out. I have to cherish all that was good. And there is so much of that. Enough for a lifetime perhaps.

Progress is amazingly quick and I am pleased with the anatomical accuracy I have achieved. Not forensically detailed, but convincing. The head is especially enjoyable to build. Eye sockets, nostrils and ears angled in such a way as to convey a noble beast. I strengthen the legs with wads of paper and tape. Marvelling at the nobbly knees. I have diverted from the model a little, due to the fact that I am unable to achieve quite the same standing position. My horse is loping forward as opposed to the more formal equestrian pose of the original. I decide to go with that as it seems to express the character of this particular animal. Friendly, empathetic.

Finally I have to think about the mane and tail, again how to convey movement. This last stage takes longer than I had expected. After a day trying to visualise exactly how horse hair behaves, I think I have got it. The mane is arranged in clumps forming a jagged edge, a bit like a steak knife although not so regular. And of course the tail has to swish. So once shaped correctly, I bind a piece of string from the tip to a chair leg. I will leave this in place overnight. That should do it.

At times like this, immersed in a project, I am aware of how odd it is to be an artist. How peculiar it is to revel in this kind of solitude especially at this time of year when all around me are homesteads groaning with cosy conviviality or at least some attempt to achieve that. The truth is I have always been this way. At times more of a curse than a blessing, right now it is, I feel, the latter.

I cannot remember a time when I didn't want to be an artist. When I wasn't an artist. There's a family story that my mother tells. Apparently we were stuck in traffic one day in Portsmouth where I grew up. It was a rather drab, grey day and I must have been in a cot or a seat in the back of the car. Suddenly the clouds cleared and according to the story, I sat bolt upright and said the word 'blue' with great excitement. She was convinced it was a sign. Certainly I have been excited by colour throughout my life, not least a blue sky. There are also many photos taken of me like some enfant sauvage, covered in paint from head to toe.

I grew up in Hampshire, where we moved around according to my parents' work. They were both classically trained musicians who had become music teachers. My mother was a pianist, my father a violinist. They had come from working-class backgrounds – my mother the child of an engineer in the Naval docks in Portsmouth, my father the son of a commercial photographer from Wales. I can remember my granny recalling how the neighbours used to crowd outside on the pavement whilst my mother, obviously talented, practised on the stand-up pianoforte in the front room. As the first generation of their respective families to go to university, education and classical music in particular had provided a passport to escape from their modest backgrounds. From the stifling restrictions of post-war Britain.

My elder brother Greg and myself were encouraged to play instruments too. I had a talent for the violin and he for the cello. For a while we formed a family string quartet. I suppose this could have been something magical but it was not. My parents were not sociable. Far from some Bohemian idyll, family life was somewhat oppressive. My father was a tortured individual, often consumed by bouts of depression. We all lived in fear of his frequent outbursts. His critiques of our performances as children could be particularly scathing. We both learnt to keep a low profile, preferring to practise our respective instruments only when he had left the house.

No doubt as a result of their musically propelled social climbing, my parents were terrible snobs. Eager to distance themselves from their roots and indeed any aspect of popular culture. In 1967 – the Summer of Love – these rather exotic people arrived on the streets of Portsmouth, as if from outer space. They had long hair, tight denims and colourful kaftans. They were hippies, hitch-hiking en route to the Isle of Wight rock festival. Of course my father utterly disapproved of them. My brother and I were not allowed to listen to pop music in the house. Quite why it disgusted him so much is still a mystery to me. Evidence it would seem of a huge insecurity on his part but perhaps not so unusual for classical musicians at the time.

Antoine Saint-Exupery famously wrote that our childhood is another country. If that's the case then mine was probably a Communist state on the wrong side of the Iron Curtain. Not feeling able to express myself or achieve any real pleasure from playing the violin, I staged my own cultural revolution and turned to art. To painting. My brother Greg, to rock music. Such is the danger of any kind of oppressive regime, namely the immense attraction of forbidden fruit to those denied the opportunity to taste it.

I can't remember precisely how old I was when I transformed my bedroom into an artist's studio, but it was ridiculously young. Three or four years old perhaps. The hub of my activities was a dilapidated free-standing kitchen cabinet with a fold-down work surface which I had sequestered from the kitchen. Those two-toned pastel-coloured forerunners of built-in kitchen units, now favoured by the shabby chic brigade. This modest facility was all I needed to enter a new world of colour and freedom. To become someone else.

If there was an artistic influence – a muse – within my family, it was my maternal grandfather, whom I adored. He had been a chief petty officer in the Navy with the good fortune of experiencing the peoples and cultures of the farthest corners of the British Empire in the 1930s. The twilight years. Latterly as a civilian, he worked as an engineering instructor in the Naval base at Gosport. He would never have considered himself an artist, yet he had a particular sensibility. An interest in creating and collecting things and, importantly, an ability to 'think out of the box'. For example, on receiving a rather beautiful photograph of a swan reflected perfectly in the glassy surface of a lake, he decided that the image would be improved by a small rotation. Thus the swan became an antelope head with antlers and remained hanging this way in his house on a permanent basis.

On his seafaring travels around the world, he had picked up all sorts of extraordinary and, to our eyes, other-worldly objects. A keen gardener in his retirement, these trophies and other interesting detritus became incorporated in various arrangements in the fecundity of his back garden in Portsmouth. Deconstruction and regeneration were very much the order of the day. If I hadn't known better I could have sworn he had studied Brancusi, particularly with reference to the totem pole formed from the disembowelling of a defunct washing machine. There was also the surprisingly successful Japanese-inspired archway, created from the framework of a Swedish armchair.

His garden was a riot of colour: lupins, red hot pokers, sunflowers and my favourite – those little pods with white flowers that burst open with one touch at the end of the summer.

It was also a place of infinite possibility both in an imaginary and a real sense. If there was a bit of welding or metalwork that needed doing, he would teach me how to do it. Similarly I learnt the rudiments of woodwork and how to deal with any number of household problems. Bird watching, bee keeping, frogs, toads and all manner of insects. Here was the universe at my feet and someone to guide me through it. He embodied a freedom and a joy that I wanted to emulate and which he encouraged. I cannot remember a time when the sun was not shining in that place.

As time spent practising the violin decreased, so time in my studio/bedroom increased until it became apparent that art was the dominant focus for me. Despite my withdrawal from the musical front line, my parents were accepting of my new vocation. As I say, they were cultural snobs and an artistic daughter was worthy of some encouragement. Deeply immersed in the process of image making, I was praised at school which gave me the confidence to enter competitions. Often advertised on the back of cereal packets with prizes galore. A Raleigh bicycle or a set of paints. Other sponsors from the grocery world included Shippam's paste and various sweet manufacturers. There is a photo of me standing proudly next to a rather clumsy oil pastel of a coal mine at the Science Museum. I must have won something.

To her credit, my mother was keen for me and my brother to visit the big museums in London. My favourite was the National Gallery where I fell in love with Van Gogh, big time. Even as a ten-year-old, I took the business of art very seriously. I have a vivid memory of standing in front of Monet's water lilies. Arms folded like a critic. Immovable. After a while I became aware of one of the attendants laughing at me. It was a kindly laugh but I suppose I must have looked ridiculous. This rather tubby little girl with a scowl on her face.

I loved the Impressionists (and still do) mainly because of the colour but also because of the world they depicted. On one level I think I wanted to climb into these paintings and escape into the society they depicted. The Paris of Seurat's *A Sunday Afternoon on the Island of La Grande Jatte* or Renoir's *Luncheon of the Boating Party*. Al fresco eating in the sunshine, by the river. Women with feathers in their hats. Bowls of peaches. All very exciting to me, coming from a world of Fray Bentos sausages and tinned peas, where scrambled eggs were unusual. Small wonder I wanted to climb on to the banks of the Seine or hang out in the salons of Montmartre.

My passion for Van Gogh bordered on obsession. This was the early 1970s. Forget 'Tiny Tears' the doll that cried and wet herself. For me it was all about Vincent. Somehow this was perfectly natural. After all, my granddad grew the most amazingly tall sunflowers. Over a period of time I developed my own technique using a combination of poster paints and yacht varnish and proceeded to give everything the Van Gogh treatment. In this way I could transform our dull back garden into a sea of romantic turbulence. Downtown Portsmouth became Arles drenched in the eternal warmth of the Mediterranean sun.

This isolated but singularly determined child is there for all to see in an essay I wrote in 1974 when I was eleven. It was my first year of secondary school. The teacher must have asked us all to tell the class about ourselves because I'd written at the top 'Introducing Myself' by Catharine Watkins, Form 1S. "I'm a quiet type of person, and happy on my own," I wrote. "I am always busy with my diary or scrapbook or doing some kind of drawing. I love sitting on the big table at home with wool, glue, paper, felt-tips and paints spread all around me."

By the early 90s, when I met Danny, it was almost twenty years since I'd written that note. I'd barely changed at all.

Part Three
SKIN

It is the end of January 2015. It is cold, damp and grey. There are days when it is impossible to imagine that the sun will ever shine again. So London remains in Christmas recovery mode, quiet, behind closed doors, which suits me. I am inhabiting my creative bubble. Industrious and inspired. "Art is the way forward," I have written in my infrequent diary and I really feel that. I am astonished at the progress I have made over the last few weeks.

I am satisfied with the form; I have been applying layer upon layer of wallpaper lining to strengthen the structure and to provide a smooth surface. I start the day by ripping up the paper into pieces about the size of a bookmark. Each layer takes ten hours or more to finish and requires three rolls from the friendly DIY shop. I leave the heating on overnight to dry it all out. It can get physically challenging. My hands have developed a rash from the wallpaper paste. I am exhausted each night, but it is restorative. I have thrown myself in at the deep end, stretching myself to the limit. An act of resurrection? The building of this thing, this beast, is opening me out rather than closing me in.

Even better, the horse is looking beautiful. Strong and sturdy. The form is accurate without being a slave to naturalism. He – for I think it is a he – has a slightly idealised, mythological quality. A friendly and yet noble creature, no doubt from a legendary land rather than some paddock in the home counties. Also, as I had hoped, there is movement, a slight leaning forward as if he is starting to trot. There is something of the ancient here. That contained energy capable of releasing itself at any moment.

Some sort of alchemy has taken place. The white lining paper has a slight sheen and glistens under the strip-lighting in the studio. It is as if I have carved this thing out of some huge block of alabaster from an Italian quarry. There is definitely something magical about this animal. I feel a strange closeness, an affection for it. And yet... I know this is not enough. A beautiful object is not enough. It is meant to tell a story of Danny and me, of our final year together. I must tell it how it is. How it was. I am daunted too because I know it will be painful. My thoughts turn to the final layer. The skin.

I have always been a little bit of a hoarder especially when it comes to things that I might be able to use for my art. Good cardboard, interesting types of paper, lengths of wood. I am also a sucker for ephemera generated by friends and family. Postcards, notes, scribbles. I have shoeboxes of them. Sentimental yes, but sometimes useful. I find handwriting particularly powerful in conjuring up time and place and also the essence of a person. A kind of DNA.

I still remember the shopping lists my granddad would write as a prelude to his frequent trips to our local Co-op store. Slightly shaky, copperplate capitals in black biro. Each item clearly delineated forming a pleasing pattern, not unlike brickwork or perhaps a more random type of masonry. Eggs, bananas, bread, steak and kidney pie, Jaffa Cakes. These items would vie with more exotic substances like Tizer or specialised cleaning fluids for buffing the brass.

We had our own language between us. For example milk would always be milluck and, for some bizarre reason, ketchup would be chicken's blood. Sadly so much of this unique language is lost to me now. It is as if we were the last members of an Amazonian tribe. Teetering on the edge of extinction. I had this special language with Danny too and so to come across fragments of intimacy in this way is incredibly moving. Not unlike the excitement an archaeologist must feel on discovering some ancient relic of Roman or Neolithic domesticity. In some ways, so much more evocative than the 'important' objects.

As a matter of habit, I had continued to collect this kind of stuff throughout my relationship with Danny. As I contemplate the final layer of the horse I know how to create it. I have the paperwork. Personal notes, prescriptions and shopping lists. Sometimes everything combined on one piece of crinkled paper. They tell the story of that last year of his life. The story I want to tell.

I begin to organise the materials at my disposal. There is a hierarchy. Personal stuff at the top going through to the more routine medical information. I am nervous. Will this work? I decide to start with the least precious collateral. The opening batch is made up of hospital discharge papers. There are a lot of these. Delicate sheets of blue and pink with perforated edges. Also in this group are the prescriptions embellished with doctors' scrawl and even harder to read in carbon-copy form. Virtually hieroglyphic in fact. There are notes from eminent consultants spouting extraordinary medical jargon: 'leo transverse colon anastomosis, metastic signet ring cell adenocarcinoma '. Signet ring? What did that mean? Was it the shape of the cancer cell? I can't remember. This was a sinister, secret language in a dialect I was incapable of mastering.

I start selecting. Tearing and cutting, taking care to preserve whole sentences or sometimes just words of particular relevance. I'm crouching under the belly of the horse. Progress is slow on this layer, partly because the papers are so delicate and also because it has to be perfect. No bubbles or creases. My thighs are aching from holding such an awkward position. From time to time the content of the material breaks through and is upsetting.

The first time I visited the chemotherapy suite at London Bridge hospital, I was shocked by the glamour of it all. Padded white leather chairs in separate cubicles, pimped-up dentists' style. Gleaming floors and nurses with spotless uniforms and perfect teeth. Due to the late diagnosis of Danny's cancer, the original tumour had already spread to the stomach lining in a spectacularly inoperable way. There was however the option of chemotherapy. Not as a cure, but to prolong life.

Glass half empty as always, Danny referred to himself as a "dead man walking". Glass half full, I began to entertain thoughts of remission. Statistics, damn statistics. Maybe we could have one last holiday together? Miami, Nice perhaps? Somewhere where treatment might be available if needed. So, replete with almost mythologically horrific stories of the possible side effects, we both decided to give it a go. I consciously employed the plural. It seemed appropriate. An attempt to tackle the loneliness of the journey that lay ahead for us both. The decision to go down this route was however most definitely not a case of 'what doesn't kill you makes you stronger...'

Five long weeks passed waiting for Danny to recover sufficiently from his emergency surgery for the treatment to begin. While the scar on his stomach healed rather well, the battle with weight loss had begun in no uncertain terms. The consumption of food sidestepped almost overnight into something fundamentally prescriptive. Pleasure, even nutrition, succumbed to a more prosaic requirement to maintain weight. Due to having had much of his colon removed, all consumption of roughage was out. And so healthy salads, fruit and curly kale gave way to streaky bacon and everything that Greggs bakery could offer. We decided to keep a joint calorie diary together. His aiming toward maximisation, mine, as ever, a battle to reach an acceptable BMI.

Life and indeed hope was becoming increasingly condensed at this point for Danny and myself. Prior to each treatment, various tests had to be undertaken to ensure his 'fitness' for the procedure. Having endured one session in considerable discomfort, the next two had to be postponed due to poor blood tests. This was hugely upsetting. As if the drawbridge had been pulled up. The walls of the castle seemingly impossible to breach. The reality of surviving outside, unknown.

The attempt at chemotherapy lasted from March through to November 2014 during which time various changes of dosage and drugs were instigated. It became apparent that Danny was only capable of receiving small doses of the required poisons thereby reducing the efficacy of the treatment. It has to be said that this punishing process had not been entirely unsuccessful. The original tumour had shrunk considerably and although I can't say I ever enjoyed our conversations, Dr Ross was a bit of a whizz with the toxins. What seeped through the cracks in the last meeting with him, was that further treatment would be futile. The cancer was taking its unstoppable course and no further treatment would stop it.

Buscopan, Ondansetron, Dexamethasone, Cyclizine Lactate and something that sounded suspiciously like Dom Perignon. The names of the drugs are so familiar to me still, like a list of cocktails at your favourite bar. Some for pain control, some to be taken before meals, some after, some for nausea. Something for every conceivable symptom. Some more effective than others. Oh yes, not forgetting Oramorph which I would carry with a handy dispenser if we ventured out.

Extraordinary to think now that the days of Danny's illness revolved around the administration of these substances either by me when he was at home or by the nursing staff when he was in hospital. His condition was volatile, so there was also the constant monitoring of temperature, frequent blood tests and white cell counts, not to mention those nights when it all went a bit pear-shaped. Why was it always three o'clock in the morning when I had to call an ambulance? Terrifying times. Pacing around the living room watching for the night duty doctor to arrive. Sometimes for hours. Danny, resisting any attempt to be moved. Sometimes shaking uncontrollably when his temperature started to rise. There was then the relief the next day, when despite feeling wrung out, I knew he was in safe hands at least until he was well enough to come home.

Throughout this period, the living room had evolved in to a medical facility of sorts. Fortunately it was a very light room with windows to the north and south. The views onto the street and across the gardens at the back provided a very welcome link to the outside world. Unlike the hermetically sealed confinement of the hospital rooms, we could enjoy the weather. The time of day, arrivals and departures. I made sure some of Danny's favourite paintings were within easy vision. An assortment of cushions were constantly arranged, rearranged and rearranged again to enable Danny to continue to work at his computer. Thinking, communicating, planning. Always with this subtle smile as he wrote emails or received messages from colleagues. The great communicator. Burnishing every word. Every sentence.

There was, unbelievably, a normalcy to it all. Things to be done. People to see. Netflix to watch. That and a growing awareness of time running out. An awareness of the end not being far away. For him, this took an active form. Relishing every ounce of enjoyment to be had out of the day. He was also enjoying the opportunity to get his affairs in order. He even mentioned to a friend that his situation wasn't so bad because he had the time to think and plan.

For me a strange seesaw of denial and the acute awareness that at some day in the near future everything would change, was a constant. Like a weary and terminally slow metronome in my head, I would think of the summer and how good it would be to sit outside together. Plant some flowers maybe? Then I would look at him working and try to imagine an empty chair. This of course was impossible.

There was a Starbucks' moment. The one nearest to Clapham Common tube station. I think it was on one of those nights when Danny was in hospital due to a problem with his white blood cell count or something, Sleep had not been easy. Once again I had woken at 4 am. I paced around for a bit until 6 am and then with a spurt of 'coping' energy I had decided to have some fresh air. Clothes quickly apportioned,

I walked purposely to the coffee shop. It was almost empty. I ordered a flat white and sat outside. The beginning of the day. All quiet. London or Clapham at least was beginning to wake up. Pavements were bubble-gum-spotted and dirty. "He is going to die," I forced myself to think. "Soon." The coffee was average and epiphanies were sorely lacking. This was not a pretty place to be. I thought about Danny and the word that he had frequently begun to use. After. Such a delicate turn of phrase. And the one that he brought into service with reference to that time when he would no longer be around. I took no comfort in the coffee, the morning air, or Danny's generous plans for my future.

So who was he, this Prince Charming? It becomes more and more difficult for me to conjure up his physical presence as time goes on. At first I could do this quite successfully. I could almost smell him. Now, that is no longer possible. At least not at will. There are moments when a sense of him will flower in my head very briefly only to disperse as I try to capture it.

I do have photographs, many of them. In books, shoeboxes, battered envelopes and on discs and devices. There is the photo reel compiled by his and my friend Rachel for the wake. This is a little tricky for me to look at now. At least the thought of it is. It is called 'Dan's slids'. I take a deep breath and insert the disc in to the computer. The screen goes momentarily black and then he's there, standing in our back garden in Cornwall. All is green and fecund, including his shirt. He is pointing towards the spindly top of a gigantic Echium. The huge triffid-like plant drills it's way upwards through a cloudless blue yonder. Another country. Might as well be another planet.

I scroll on. Lots of childhood scenes in black and white. Mainly group shots of him with his brothers and sisters. Sean, Julie, Lizzy, Helen and Sarah. Standing in a row. Their faces are variations on a theme. Some round, some more oval in shape. They're skinny with pudding bowl haircuts. Danny has the biggest ears and the biggest grin. Often, Tommy, the father, is standing in the centre of the group. He is lean and rangy with a boxer's face and arms. About as Irish as you could imagine and a bit of a snappy dresser. He wasn't a boxer, but was more than capable of a few moves. His working life was chequered. Originally from Waterford, he had at one time joined the police force but for the most part, worked in factories in West London. A compulsive poet, he wrote rhyming verse on a daily basis. Two themes prevailed, his love for the family and his Catholic faith. Not troubled by material ambition, he was however fond of the gee-gees which I think must have been a little stressful for Danny's mother Mavis at times.

A nurse by profession and clearly in charge of the camera, there are less images of her. One of the few photos of them all together looks like it was taken at a holiday camp. Perhaps they purchased it? Mavis is wearing those wacky fifties butterfly wing specs. Tommy is leaning in on the shot. Hair slicked back and gleaming. A lady in a piny with a large embroidered B on the pocket is wielding an oversized chrome tea pot in dangerous proximity to Danny and Sean. Happy days I suspect.

There is something of the pioneering spirit in these captured moments. Wagons rollin'. This was however West London, as opposed to anything wilder. Acton to be precise. Perhaps it is just the black and whiteness of them or perhaps it is the implied poverty and my knowledge of what a struggle it was for Tommy and Mavis to look after their brood. These were difficult times after the war. Housing was in very short supply and I should imagine it was sometimes impossible to make ends meet.

Mavis as ever was very focused on education. As luck would have it, an opportunity came to light through one of Tommy's workmates at the Hoover factory. Apparently there was a school down in Sussex that would take on bright kids and educate them for free. This school was called Christ's Hospital.

I'm scrolling forward. Danny is now running through the countryside. He must be fourteen or fifteen. Still skinny, his hair is longer now and he is wearing a rugby shirt. There he is again, in a group shot in the back row. He is wearing that distinctive uniform, I think it is sixteenth century or thereabouts. It consists of a heavy frock coat over knee britches, fastened at the front with silver buttons. There is also a rather flouncy neck tie and some extraordinary mustard-coloured socks. These were apparently to frighten the rats.

To cut a long story short, both Danny and his brother were to pass the entrance exam for Christ's Hospital and went on to receive an amazing education there. Clearly a life changing opportunity for them both and one that Danny cherished with ever increasing fondness. This was the place where his intelligence, ambition and ethical code crystallised into what was to become his unique contribution to the charity sector. Sean also did well as an orthopaedic surgeon. The fly in the ointment was perhaps the stipulation that only the first two children of any family could apply, leaving Danny's sisters to fend for themselves in Acton.

Back to the photo reel and I am navigating my way through a seemingly endless catalogue of celebratory events, most of which depict Danny and myself in various states of drunkenness. I guess that is when pictures are taken. There are gaps though. What about Killing Joke?

After a rather undistinguished spell at Durham University – possibly theology wasn't the best choice – Danny took up residence in a series of squats in Holland Park, London. This was of course the breeding ground for the music industry at the time. I am uncertain of exactly how it happened but somehow, Danny became part of the management team for a punk band called Killing Joke. Thus the entrepreneur in him had found some traction and suddenly the world was a smaller place. I have one photo from then. Danny is lurking in the background of a recording session, I think it was for John Peel. He was as ever, more than happy to be in the background.

Family snaps of this period depict Danny at weddings wearing rakish suits and shades. Indoors. The photographic record continues to be sketchy until his wedding to his first wife June in the early eighties. Here, June is chic and stylish, dwarfed by Danny in a questionable shiny shirt and bowtie combo. They both look very much in love. Married for ten years, there's was an eventful union. Highs, lows and every stage in between. Perhaps the age difference was a problem. He was ten years younger. Eventually, whatever glue they had at the beginning, ceased to hold them together and they parted. Danny remained committed to June and her children Alex and Lydia for the rest of his life.

It's a cruel business the music industry. After the implosion of Killing Joke, Danny's attempts to pursue a career in the music industry met with little success and some considerable financial distress. Never a stranger to earning a living, he at first turned his hand to mini cab driving before accepting a job selling advertising space for a publishing company. In an alarmingly short space of time he outgrew the sales department to become an editor, initially of that historic publication, *Pigeon Post*. A favourite of the late Queen Mother as Danny would frequently inform me. There followed time on a magazine called

Balloon Europe before he seized the opportunity to launch *Balloon World* under his own banner.

Once the captain of his ship, Danny began to evolve in to what was to become his mature identity as a publisher and what I can only describe as the 'black tie' years on the photo reel. Clearly something had been fermenting in him. A focus and a perception way beyond the parameters of the entertainment business, or indeed pigeons. Able and empowered, he began to channel his considerable energies in a new direction. Namely, his burgeoning fascination with the not-for-profit sector.

At the age of thirty-two, he launched a magazine called *Assembly and Association*. This was a forum for representative and membership bodies. He went on to found *Fundraising* which was the UK's first ever magazine in that field. In 1990 he established what was to become Civil Society Media and to publish *NGO Finance*, latterly *Charity Finance*. It was all a case of Danny knowing what charities needed to know and how to deliver it to them. How he could help charities do better.

To this end, his drive for work was exceptional. There is a great photo of him at his desk circa 1990. He is bent over, writing something by hand. His overly long fringe hides most of his face and he is further obscured by a wall of box files and papers. An example of a rare species caught unawares? Disturbance was not encouraged in this, his natural habitat. I might wish that he had not worked so hard, but that wouldn't have been him.

Time off wasn't really on. Certainly not for the first decade of our relationship. With the passage of time, weekends did make something of a comeback. Typically, Saturdays were given over to hunter-gatherer mode. Good food would be purchased and sometimes additions to his wardrobe would be considered. He had inherited something of Tommy's way in a sartorial sense. Often the afternoon would involve art. I would be tasked with selecting something good to see. Danny was broad-minded and sophisticated in his love of painting in particular. He collected naïve art but also nurtured a passion for British Modernism. A good Victor Pasmore or anything by Milton Avery could and would reduce him to tears.

Once home, I would set too with the ingredients and attempt to satisfy the very high bar set by him. He was something of a perfectionist, to put it mildly. I love cooking, so this was a joy for me, if a little demanding. Danny would tolerate my addiction to trash TV, pretending to ignore the latest talent show from behind the *Financial Times* or some scuffed volume of Thackery. George Eliot was his favourite. I think he enjoyed the trash TV too.

Walking was important. Around St Ives in Cornwall, or the 'hood in Camberwell. In fact, walking and talking with him is probably one of the things I miss the most. His unique stream of commentary on the world. Local, global, funny, serious. Our shared history. There is a deafening silence now when I return to those haunts. And also when anything interesting happens. What would he have thought?

There is a moment when the word 'palliative' enters the arena. Once the chemo had ended we found ourselves in something of a vacuum. Certainly the freedom from the enforced poisonings was a relief. Thinking about what lay ahead, less so. Friends were informed that the original tumour had diminished greatly. The fact that the disease was advancing in other areas was less easy to communicate. I don't think we tried very hard to do that.

The idea was that Danny would stay at home for as long as possible, hopefully to the end.

We had previously visited a couple of local hospices. Heart-breaking afternoons. Sitting in waiting rooms on comfortable chairs. The calm of the staff. Beautiful flowers. Soft voices. Tears.

A home care plan was put in place consisting of teams of nurses arriving throughout the day to monitor pain control and other key measurements. In an attempt to preserve some privacy and homeliness at least at the start of the day, I volunteered to do the first shift. Not being natural nursing material, I carried out my duties quaking under Danny's hawk eyes. Following the written instructions to the letter, we achieved something like hospital-standard hygiene and rigour, literally on pain of death. Any infections could have been fatal. Extraordinary furniture was provided including a giant fridge and a motorised mattress lift that could angle the bed at the touch of a button. I looked forward to the frequent visits from Joyce, the head nurse, who embodied all that is powerful and kind in equal measure.

I have kept those notes pertaining to my nursing duties. Pencil scribbles with numbered actions, detailing the precise methods to sterilise syringes and how to check for air blocks in the intravenous tubing. The mid-section of the horse is almost completely covered. Its white belly now a swathe of pink and blue. I need the horse to tell a story, in such a way that is comprehensible. Not a confusing mess of references. Perhaps the way to do this is to group materials relating to particular episodes in certain areas. I decide to attach all the shopping lists for example on the rump, the home care stuff on the neck and so on. I must not forget that I want the horse to convey more than Danny's cancer journey. It needs to evoke the life that was going on before and during the dreaded routine of hospital appointments and treatments. Our personal life.

What to do with the bundle of Valentine's cards? I find my final Christmas card from him. It says "to my darling wife Catharine. Christmas 2015." He had in fact got the year wrong. It was Christmas 2014 when he wrote it. Had he meant it to count for two years, the second one a posthumous greeting? A message in a bottle.

The originals are too precious to be tampered with so I photocopy them on my printer upstairs. Making sure that the words are fully legible, I tear the photocopied sheets into strips and apply them to the left-hand shoulder of the horse. Here I am, in the barely warm enough studio wearing a glue-splattered tracksuit over thermal leggings. There is a note scribbled in thick black pen. It says "get married" in Danny's handwriting. That was eight months ago.

It was barely eight in the morning of 28th May 2015 and I had already successfully managed to burn one tray of thinly sliced bread. Thankfully I had bought two French sticks just in case. I had already consigned the charred slices to the bin and begun attempting to grill another batch. Thankfully too, Danny was out of the way, upstairs getting dressed. By the time he arrived downstairs the culinary crisis would be over.

The big day was upon us which was something of a miracle in itself. The past couple of months had been eventful to say the least and I had become accustomed to the possibility that it would never happen. In and out of the intensive care unit, Danny had endured a variety of setbacks. A clot on the lung, the threat of an embolism and also a few bouts of suspected septicaemia. Oh yes, and we were told that the tumours were growing. Nevertheless, he was on good form today. The day of our wedding.

Various platters arranged and appropriate herbs sprinkled, I quickly got dressed. Feeling suitably attired in a hasty concoction of high street purchases, I then embarked on possibly the biggest challenge of the day, how to apply my rather fetching midnight blue fascinator with something approaching dignity.

I had just returned to the kitchen, headdress in place, when Danny descended the stairs. Always something of a clothes horse, his recently purchased Issey Miyake jacket with its cut-off collar brought out something of the Cuban revolutionary in him. His weight loss had also served to bolster a distinct resemblance to Bill Nighy. He looked great.

Like latter-day versions of Johnny and Fanny Craddock, we continued to fuss over the breakfast. A feast of Cornish lobster and Newlyn Bay crab, both delivered the previous day from a trusted supplier in Newlyn. Released from the intensive care unit to which he had been consigned only two days previously, Danny busied himself – as was his habit – with checking the temperature of the champagne and the glasses into which it would shortly be decanted.

Due to the volatility of his condition, a 'big' wedding had of course been out of the question. "Would he be alive on the day?" So we awaited a select group of guests; Rachel, John and Alex. It was a little before ten-thirty when they arrived, already having eaten breakfast it appeared. It was soon clear that I had prepared way too much food, but this did nothing to dampen Danny's mood. He was on fire, buzzing with energy, no doubt as a result of a couple of dexamethasone tablets – dexies as Danny fondly referred to them. His oncologist had advised him against taking them but, I suspect drawing on his former life in the music business, it was a case of 'whatever gets you through the night'. Particularly when you are trying to deal with stage four bowel cancer.

The ceremony was set for twelve noon. A little after eleven-thirty we headed off for the short walk to Camberwell registry office. All five of us were wearing red roses, held in place by silver lapel brooches we had acquired on eBay. The weather was dry but slightly cloudy. Acceptable. At least it was not raining.

Danny's most recent proposal to me had been delivered as he lay on a hospital gurney minutes before being wheeled away for the stomach operation back in January. My response had, as ever, been less than affirmative. I do not consider myself a romantic and am inclined to display an anti-establishment streak when cornered. Thus I never felt the need to cement our relationship by getting married. Given the circumstances, however, I had undergone a change of heart. I wanted to please him, to honour his wishes. He had a sensible point, of course. Happy to assure anyone and everyone that he married for love, the organiser in him was also anxious to ensure that I would be protected legally and financially after his death. It was, I learned later, far from unusual for this kind of marriage to take place. In the brief run-up to our big day, we had discussed the possibility of the ceremony taking place in the hospital if necessary. We were told that they had held several that week already.

With our intimate wedding party assembled and on time, the short ceremony proceeded without a hitch. In keeping with our neighbourhood in Camberwell, it was friendly and more than a little eccentric. Even the registrar had to laugh when, halfback way through the proceedings, Danny took a call on his mobile from the taxi firm he had booked to take us to lunch.

After a few appropriate photos in the beautiful rose garden behind the ever-so-crumbling Georgian splendour of the registry office, we were soon on our way to Trinity, Danny's favourite restaurant in Clapham. A magnificent lunch was had by all as they say. The 'dexies' seemed to do wonders for Danny's appetite. When I look back on the photos of that day I am immensely comforted. Danny had never looked so happy. It was as if there had been nothing to blight our lives. As if we had everything to live for.

I start early. Coffee and bagel in hand, progress is good. By lunchtime I have achieved total coverage. The horse has a skin. I sit back on my Mastermind chair and take it in. "Hmmm. I'm not sure." I get up and walk around. I examine from close up, at a distance, from the side, even climbing onto a small step ladder to take an aerial view. "Hmmm." I step away. Another cup of coffee. A square of dark chocolate. Anything to ease the mounting panic, because now I'm not sure. "It's not working."

The beautiful white creature is now swathed in an ugly patina of incomprehensible typed text. The paperwork is supposed to convey an inherent emotional charge. My intention had been that it would irradiate the form of the horse. That meaning would be bestowed as if touched by the magic wand of truth. This isn't happening. It is ugly. Lifeless. I feel sick. The elation of the past four weeks collapses like a row of deckchairs in the wind. I sit in my Mastermind chair, turning in small, ten degree motions, from side to side. So why would a sculpture of a white horse covered in medical notes work anyway? Why didn't I realise this earlier? It was a crap idea. A dud.

I spend the next few hours attempting to distract myself with worthy pursuits. I wash up. I do two loads of laundry. I go to Sainsbury's and buy some healthy food. By lunchtime I can avoid the situation no longer and I return to the studio. The horse looks just as bad. I feel doubly bereft. How can I rescue it and myself?

Sometimes when you are breaking new ground you have to release yourself from judgement. That internal voice that is observing, measuring and yes judging your every move. You have to trust your instincts to let you know when it rings true. Or doesn't, as the case may be. It is about throwing the net a little wider than you have ever done before. Exploring unchartered territory. A sculpture of this scale and ambition is new ground for me so the normal rules haven't applied. My radar has failed me. I blame my emotional state as much as anything. Perhaps it has all been an epic distraction, an elaborate ploy to circumnavigate my grief?

I can feel myself sinking. The alarm bells are ringing. I can get depressed and panicky when my efforts come to nothing. I must watch out for that. I have more than enough to deal with as it is, without some creative meltdown. I'm looking for a lifeline. I tell myself that I have been here before. Experience is everything. I remember previous works, previous wrong turns. And the solutions. I am reminded that sometimes the best art, the art that has the greatest potency, has to be rescued. There has to be an element of jeopardy mixed with discovery. You have to break the mould to get some energy into something. They say that about writing too. What's that horrible expression? 'Kill your children.' Sometimes you have to take out your favourite sentence to make it work. To tell the story better. That's what I need to do. Or something like that. I will not give up yet. I need to hang on in there. Be patient. Keep destructive thoughts at bay. Make room in my head for further recalibrations to occur. I need to feel that there is hope.

Creative endeavours are often about displacement. Distracting yourself with other pursuits and allowing the subconscious to crank through the gears, to work it all out. And so for the next day or two I busy myself with cleaning, tidying, organising. Every now and again I step back into the studio and look at the horse. It still depresses me.

It's early evening a few days later. I am pretending to myself that I don't care, that there is so much more to my life even in widowhood, than this bloody horse. Sitting, swivelling in my chair I notice that on the head there is a particularly dense patch of bold type which from a distance looks like a spot or a smudge. It has created the dappled effect you might find on certain breeds of white horses. Not necessarily piebald or skewbald with their white and black and brown spots, just a sort of faded patchiness. I look it up. The most famous breed of grey or white horse is a Lipizzaner. Born any colour, they progressively lighten with age until they are pure white. Perhaps my horse can be a young adult still in the process of becoming alabaster white? Perhaps the text can perform a visual function as well as a narrative one. It has to, in fact. But how?

I am talking to myself and beginning to sense a shift in my understanding of what is happening. Here is a three-dimensional object. Therefore the words – important as they are – have to be intrinsic to the physical properties of the sculpture. They have to add to the horsiness of the horse if you like. Currently the text is not relating to the horse at all, it is merely a covering.

I have an idea. Without obscuring their meaning, I think I need to bring out the purely visual impact of the letters and words. The abstract qualities. Density, tonality, scale. Perhaps this is not just a sculpture, it is a three-dimensional drawing? I decide to experiment with a small portion of the head. "Let's see if it works here. Let's not risk the whole thing."

I return to my collection of ephemera. On the top of one pile of papers is an A4 sheet. Notes from a meeting with a consultant. It is in Danny's hand and true to form, replete with doodles. Intense balls of blue biro interspersed with jagged, triangular constructions. He was famous for his doodles. They appear like contagious rashes throughout most of his diaries and handwritten papers. Bingo! I think to myself. Let's try a few of these.

Barely able to control my excitement I apply a few of the biro circles to the head of the horse. Next I add a few scribbles from my diary written in thick black felt-tipped pen. One says "V, V tired" Another "D, vomiting again". I step back towards the chair, but don't sit down. I want to observe it from a little closer. The additions look like random markings but they also look naturalistic. The whole surface has become more animated by the mix of legible and illegible words and shapes. They have integrated together successfully. They can coexist. I am too afraid to say it out loud, but I see grounds for optimism, some light. This might be OK. It might be the way forward. And, even better, if it is, it is Danny's hand that has made it work.

Finally I can relax. The butterflies have left my stomach. Over the next few days I carefully apply more of my precious collection of ephemera to the body of the horse, taking care not to obscure meaning in the service of achieving an improved visual effect. On the tail, I decide to do something a little different. I want to celebrate Danny's professional achievements. His qualities as perceived by his colleagues and peers. For this, I deconstruct pages from the condolence book made in his honour. Extracts like "a true gent", "an exceptional person", creative, warm, funny, and "no frills". All seem appropriate to inform the defiant swish of the horse's tail.

It is about a week later and after some hesitation and many reworkings of different parts, I finally feel that I am where I want to be. All that remains is to do something with the stand. I can hardly believe that in a mere seven weeks the horse had come to life. I feel elated and at the same time bereft. in a new way. Since Christmas Eve I have been totally consumed by the project. I have climbed a mountain. Physically, emotionally and artistically. I have not felt alone. Without a doubt Danny's doodles saved the day. We did this together.

Another cup of coffee. I am walking around the horse. Feeling good. Reading extracts from various sections. "D. glad to be home", "Bananas, Buscopan, more morphine", "overall he is feeling better", "ring community nurses", "peach cordial", "prescription to chemists", "v v v tired", "out of hours numbers". My thoughts turn to what was going on almost exactly a year ago.

There had come a point when due to the obstructions in his colon, Danny could no longer eat and so food had to be supplied intravenously. This development required further hospitalisation of our already over-crowded living room predominantly in the form of a huge medicalised fridge for nutritional supplements.

Having eaten his last meal, I became embarrassed by food adverts on TV and the seemingly endless cookery programmes. Danny was not bothered, concentrating instead on how to achieve the perfect ice cube. Thus his foodie predilections refocused on to this new specialism. I seem to remember that ice cubes left in a jug of water in the fridge for approximately 30 minutes were best. Woe betide anyone who attempted to serve him any other kind.

The period from mid-December 2014 through to mid-January 2015 was, on reflection, the last lap. A gradual physical shutting down had begun although not in any sense pertaining to Danny's mental state which remained in tip-top condition. The incredible machinery of his brain presiding without any noticeable difference, over the crumbling dysfunctionality of his body. He continued to work.

His focus on enjoyment and how we could enjoy ourselves together was undiminished. Unable to eat, he decided that it might be possible to hang out in cocktail bars instead of restaurants. He would regrettably be sticking to water. "But would they make the right ice cubes?" I asked.

Unfortunately, we never made it onto the cocktail circuit. Danny died in his sleep on the morning of February 9th 2015. A couple of days later I received a heart-shaped box of chocolates from a very expensive chocolatier. Just in time for Valentine's day. Inside was a printed card:

More fun required! Dxxx

Epilogue
SUMMER 2016

I have decided to have a gathering in the sunshine, in the garden. So that people can meet the horse. The flowers are bright and the air is soft, suffused with barbecue smoke. There is laughter, the clinking of glasses. There are sausages. A bunch of staff from Danny's publishing company are tucking into the beer. I have slipped into the familiar 'hostess with the mostess' role. I want this to be a celebration.

With the help of my friends Peter and Jo, I have carefully wheeled the sculpture out from the studio, positioning it in the furthest corner of the garden where the sun will pick it out. It looks striking. Filled with coltish energy. As if it has been reined in and is now excited to be set free. It might bound over the wall and run off at any moment. I wouldn't hold it back, but I'd miss it. I feel an intense affection for this sculpture, more than I have towards anything else I have created.

People are responding warmly. A woman is talking about Barbara Hepworth. I notice that one or two guests are being reticent. They are standing at a safe distance, five or six strides away, so that the details aren't too immediate. If they do look closely it is only fleetingly, as if leaning into and then withdrawing from a fire, afraid of being licked by the flames. I think it is the intimacy that is daunting. Or is it death itself? They are all friends or colleagues of mine and Danny. People who were with us during his illness in one way or another. I suspect they fear the potency of what is being revealed. I try to reassure them. A little too much perhaps. Jollity can so easily tip into hysteria. There is actually no need for them to be afraid. There is nothing here but the truth.

The day feels like an end and a beginning. As an artist, I think you set a task in relation to the depth of thought or volume of feeling that you are trying to communicate. Mine were not small goals. My grief was Gothic and melodramatic – there were extremes going on. Life-changing would seem an inadequate tag. I also felt it needed to be a big statement for Danny. A match for him. So I am verging on ecstatic that I have achieved this, done something that I thought was going to be impossible.

I really didn't think I could do it. I saw too many limitations. My inexperience as a sculptor. The physical and technical challenges, especially at the start. "I don't even know how to make it stand up." But the boundaries had just evaporated around me. They had ceased to exist. Because the worst had already happened. It was just like jumping into the deep end without arm bands. I probably needed some deeply immersive experience.

Now, at the end of it all, I feel I have relived every twist and turn of our final year together. A resurrection of sorts has taken place. But what now? I realise that an emptying out has occurred. What had been so dense inside – as dense as concrete or the thickest forest – is now lighter. I have created some space internally. Some room to manoeuvre. I feel the possibility of change. Where do I want to go?

I am sadder certainly. Significantly so, but also with some weirdly enhanced capacity for joy. Witnessing death is surely the best cure for everyday neurosis. There are moments when I border on a kind of evangelical high. I have this new respect for my life, that and the need to live for Danny too. To enjoy the day for him and to continue to make each day the best it can be. Another form of holding on to him I guess, but it suits me for the present.

The grief 'journey' has been exhausting and surprising too. One of those experiences that is nigh on impossible to communicate to the uninitiated. Like being a member of a secret club. I have had some amazing support from friends and also some frustration with what has been expected of me. As a widow. Crying too much or not enough? Time to 'move on' or not? Should I still have all those photos in the living room? I suspect some friends think not. And the clothes in the wardrobe. I haven't sorted them out yet.

Many people are too scared to mention 'it' – the death. For fear of upsetting me or is it themselves? That crying thing again. There is an awkwardness about it all. Far too much at stake for small talk. Consequently, there are times when it is so much easier to talk to strangers. There was the lady at the drycleaners who had also lost her husband. The young woman on the train who had lost her fiancé. Then there was George the plumber.

George and his workmate Az are particularly good at fixing boilers. Early in the spring of 2016, the clapped-out boiler that serves to heat the studio gave up on me. Fortunately George was at hand to come to the rescue. After some hours of high-level intervention on his part, I made him a cup of tea and we got talking about Danny. And about death. I showed him the horse.

"The thing is," I said, "what happens to all that energy? Those electrical connections in the brain? Because of course Danny was totally compos mentis until the end and the thing I can't get my head around is what happens to that. Where does it go? I can understand the body failing, but the intellect, the spirit, that's something else. It made me think of the London Palladium and standing on that stage so many years ago. There was a feeling. Something 'electric'. Even in the afternoon when nothing was happening. There was a charge in that place, from human activity. Everything that had gone on before."

We then proceeded to have a long and very interesting conversation aided in no small part by the fact that George is a very intelligent and philosophical kind of person.

"The thing is Cathy," he replied, "directional energy doesn't stop. Ever. It just gets transmitted. An electrical charge – whether it's from lightning or something else – it transmits to another entity or host."

We then proceeded to talk about other things. His blues band. The weather. It was a great conversation and one that helped me enormously at the time and to this day.

I like to think of art or being creative, in terms of a currency, an unstoppable force. All that energy is like the flow of a river after heavy rain. Carving out new channels and directions, passing through new territories. Things that are stuck can become unstuck.

And what of the future? I suppose without consciously recognising it, 'the future' before Danny's illness had taken the form of a road or pathway along which we would progress together. It would be punctuated with travel, art, time with friends and family. Fun, struggle, boredom, stress. All part of a familiar human landscape with a visible yet distant horizon. There is now instead a pool. A deep dark pool which is beautiful, but at the same time, unsettling. Everything lies in those waters and the smallest stone thrown into it sets off a thousand ripples, an effect so penetrating it is more like a sound reverberating deep inside my head. There is no discernible shape or certainty going forward, but I am not overwhelmed by that. In fact I find the lack of definition, positive.

Bring on the mystery. I am not so afraid anymore.

Lightning Source UK Ltd.
Milton Keynes UK
UKHW010633130122
397082UK00002B/277